Kemp

by Iain Gray

WRITING to REMEMBER

LangSyne
PUBLISHING
WRITING *to* REMEMBER

79 Main Street, Newtongrange,
Midlothian EH22 4NA
Tel: 0131 344 0414   Fax: 0845 075 6085
E-mail: info@lang-syne.co.uk
www.langsyneshop.co.uk

Design by Dorothy Meikle
Printed by Printwell Ltd
© Lang Syne Publishers Ltd 2021

All rights reserved. No part of this publication may be reproduced, stored or introduced into a retrieval system, or transmitted in any form or by any means (electronic, mechanical, photocopying, recording or otherwise) without the prior written permission of Lang Syne Publishers Ltd.

ISBN 978-1-85217-786-7

Kemp

MOTTO:
I hope for light

CREST:
A falcon

NAME variations include:
Kempe

Chapter one:

The origins of popular surnames

by George Forbes and Iain Gray

***If you don't know where you came from, you won't know where you're going* is a frequently quoted observation and one that has a particular resonance today when there has been a marked upsurge in interest in genealogy, with increasing numbers of people curious to trace their family roots.**

Main sources for genealogical research include census returns and official records of births, marriages and deaths – and the key to unlocking the detail they contain is obviously a family surname, one that has been 'inherited' and passed from generation to generation.

No matter our station in life, we all have a surname – but it was not until about the middle of the fourteenth century that the practice of being identified by a particular surname became commonly established throughout the British Isles.

Previous to this, it was normal for a person to be identified through the use of only a forename.

But as population gradually increased and there were many more people with the same forename, surnames were adopted to distinguish one person, or community, from another.

Many common English surnames are patronymic in origin, meaning they stem from the forename of one's father – with 'Johnson,' for example, indicating 'son of John.'

It was the Normans, in the wake of their eleventh century conquest of Anglo-Saxon England, a pivotal moment in the nation's history, who first brought surnames into usage – although it was a gradual process.

For the Normans, these were names initially based on the title of their estates, local villages and chateaux in France to distinguish and identify these landholdings.

Such grand descriptions also helped enhance the prestige of these warlords and generally glorify their lofty positions high above the humble serfs slaving away below in the pecking order who had only single names, often with Biblical connotations as in Pierre and Jacques.

The only descriptive distinctions among the peasantry concerned their occupations, like 'Pierre the swineherd' or 'Jacques the ferryman.'

Roots of surnames that came into usage in England not only included Norman-French, but also Old French, Old Norse, Old English, Middle English, German, Latin, Greek, Hebrew and the Gaelic languages of the Celts.

The Normans themselves were originally Vikings, or 'Northmen', who raided, colonised and eventually settled down around the French coastline.

They had sailed up the Seine in their longboats in 900AD under their ferocious leader Rollo and ruled the roost in north eastern France before sailing over to conquer England in 1066 under Duke William of Normandy – better known to posterity as William the Conqueror, or King William I of England.

Granted lands in the newly-conquered England, some of their descendants later acquired territories in Wales, Scotland and Ireland – taking not only their own surnames, but also the practice of adopting a surname, with them.

But it was in England where Norman rule and custom first impacted, particularly in relation to the adoption of surnames.

This is reflected in the famous *Domesday Book*, a massive survey of much of England and Wales, ordered by William I, to determine who owned what, what it was worth and therefore how much they were liable to pay in taxes to the voracious Royal Exchequer.

Completed in 1086 and now held in the National Archives in Kew, London, 'Domesday' was an Old English word meaning 'Day of Judgement.'

This was because, in the words of one contemporary chronicler, "its decisions, like those of the Last Judgement, are unalterable."

It had been a requirement of all those English landholders – from the richest to the poorest – that they identify themselves for the purposes of the survey and for future reference by means of a surname.

This is why the *Domesday Book*, although written in Latin as was the practice for several centuries with both civic and ecclesiastical records, is an invaluable source for the early appearance of a wide range of English surnames.

Several of these names were coined in connection with occupations.

These include Baker and Smith, while Cooks, Chamberlains, Constables and Porters were to be found carrying out duties in large medieval households.

The church's influence can be found in names such as Bishop, Friar and Monk while the popular name of Bennett derives from the late fifth to mid-sixth century Saint Benedict, founder of the Benedictine order of monks.

The early medical profession is represented by Barber, while businessmen produced names that include Merchant and Sellers.

Down at the village watermill, the names that cropped up included Millar/Miller, Walker and Fuller, while other self-explanatory trades included Cooper, Tailor, Mason and Wright.

Even the scenery was utilised as in Moor, Hill, Wood and Forrest – while the hunt and the chase supplied names that include Hunter, Falconer, Fowler and Fox.

Colours are also a source of popular surnames, as in Black, Brown, Gray/Grey, Green and White, and would have denoted the colour of the clothing the person habitually wore or, apart from the obvious exception of 'Green', one's hair colouring or even complexion.

The surname Red developed into Reid, while

Blue was rare and no-one wanted to be associated with yellow.

Rather self-important individuals took surnames that include Goodman and Wiseman, while physical attributes crept into surnames such as Small and Little.

Many families proudly boast the heraldic device known as a Coat of Arms, as featured on our front cover.

The central motif of the Coat of Arms would originally have been what was borne on the shield of a warrior to distinguish himself from others on the battlefield.

Not featured on the Coat of Arms, but highlighted on page three, is the family motto and related crest – with the latter frequently different from the central motif.

Adding further variety to the rich cultural heritage that is represented by surnames is the appearance in recent times in lists of the 100 most common names found in England of ones that include Khan, Patel and Singh – names that have proud roots in the vast sub-continent of India.

Echoes of a far distant past can still be found in our surnames and they can be borne with pride in commemoration of our forebears.

Chapter two:

Angels and demons

A surname of truly martial roots, 'Kemp' derives from the Middle English 'kempe' that, in turn, stems from the Saxon, or Old English, 'cempa', descriptive of a warrior or champion.

In particular, it refers to a soldier or man-at-arms proficient in hand-to-hand combat, such as in jousting, while in the sense of 'struggle' its German counterpart is 'kamp' and, meaning 'striving', lends itself to the Old Scots 'kemping' descriptive of the hard manual toil of reaping a field during harvest.

Found throughout the British Isles from earliest times, the name is not confined to any particular English county, although the first historical reference appears in Wiltshire in the now redundant form 'Cempa', where an Eadulf Cempa is recorded in 902.

Despite its military connotations, its early bearers came to attention through many different pursuits – including not only the Church but also in the mysterious realms of the supernatural and witchcraft.

The son of a prominent Kentish family, John Kemp was the churchman and diplomat who rose to become Archbishop of Canterbury.

Born in about 1380 at the family home of Olantigh, in the parish of Wye, an indication of his status is that his father Thomas is described as a 'gentleman', while his mother Beatrix was daughter of a Sir Thomas Lewkenor.

Educated at Merton College, Oxford and trained as an ecclesiastical lawyer, he entered royal service in about 1415 as an administrator, later chancellor, of what was then the English duchy of Normandy.

Returning to his native land, his rise through the church hierarchy was rapid, holding positions that included Archdeacon of Durham, Bishop of Rochester and Archbishop of York.

Complementing these powerful Church offices, he was entrusted with royal appointments including Keeper of the Privy Seal and with diplomatic missions to France – while all the while managing to chart a precarious course through the complex political machinations of his time.

Appointed Archbishop of Canterbury two years before his death in 1454, one of his legacies was the foundation of Wye College, which remained part of the University of London until its closure in 2009.

Extreme religious passion can often manifest itself in bizarre fashion, and no less so than in the particularly incredulous Middle Ages.

Author of what is recognised as the first autobiography written in the English language, Margery Kempe (at this period the forms 'Kemp' and 'Kempe' appear interchangeable) was the married name of the Christian mystic Margery Burnham, or Brunham, born in about 1373 in what was then Bishop's Lynn, Norfolk, now King's Lynn.

The daughter of a merchant who was also mayor of the town, she was aged about 20 when she married local man John Kempe and the couple went on to have at least fourteen children together – despite Margery's frequently heralded wish to live a chaste life.

After the birth of her first child she began to experience strange visions in which she claimed demons attacked and ordered her to abandon her faith – but these were offset by other revelations of angels and saints and even one where she apparently miraculously witnessed the birth of Christ and also his crucifixion.

Given to bouts of loud weeping, wailing and

prayer in expiation of her perceived sins, she appears to have become something of an embarrassing nuisance and was imprisoned for a time by the clerical authorities.

It may have been somewhat of a relief to the good townsfolk when she frequently took herself off on pilgrimage to holy sites not only in England but also much further afield including Santiago de Compostello, in Spain, and also the Holy Land – experiencing celestial visions along the way.

In about the early 1430s, and being illiterate, she dictated her 'spiritual autobiography' to a scribe and this, about twelve years after her death in 1438, was copied and transcribed again as *The Book of Margery Kempe*.

Excerpts were published in about 1501 and then again in 1521, but it was not until 1934 that the only surviving full manuscript was found in a private library.

Recognised as the first autobiography written in the English language and frequently republished and translated into other languages, it provides a fascinating insight into not only Margery Kempe's mystical experiences but also the lives and times of women in general during the period.

In the midst of the sixteenth century hysteria over a demonic conspiracy to ensnare the souls of Christians and visit torments upon them, Ursula Kemp was the English healer and midwife hanged along with five others for witchcraft.

Also recorded as 'Ursley Kempe' and 'Ursley Grey' and born in about 1525 in the village of St Osyth, Essex, she was known locally as a 'cunning woman' – skilled in the arts of healing, or folk medicine.

This was sometimes through resort to harmless rituals and incantations deemed 'magical' – but when practitioners such as Ursula Kemp fell foul of their neighbours for whatever petty reason, this 'magic' was enough to condemn them as witches in league with the Devil and his hellish legion of demons.

Tried for witchcraft at Chelmsford in February of 1582 before Justice Brian Darcy, it was alleged by her neighbour Grace Thurlow that she had caused the death of her infant daughter, made her son ill and herself lame.

This occurred, Thurlow claimed, after she and Kemp had argued over payment the latter had demanded for previous treatment she had administered to her ailing son.

Alice Letherdale, another neighbour with whom she had argued, claimed she had exacted dire revenge by bewitching her daughter Elizabeth to death.

Also accused of having maliciously caused the death of Edna Stratton, even her eight-year-old son Thomas was induced to testify against her.

His mother, he claimed, kept four spirits, or familiars – a black cat called Jacke, a grey one named Tyffin, a black toad known as Dygine and Tyttey, a white lamb.

These familiars, the lad said, were given cake and beer and allowed to suck blood from her body.

Justice Darcy meanwhile claimed that, before her trial proper, Kemp had made a 'private confession' of witchcraft – whether extracted through torture or other physical duress is unclear.

At the very least it would have involved sleep deprivation and semi-starvation that would have brought on hallucinations.

A number of years previously, she is alleged to have told Darcy, she had suffered 'lameness in her bones' and sought out a cunning woman for a cure.

The woman told her she had been bewitched and to 'unwitch' herself she should use a noxious ritual involving various herbs and hog's dung.

She also confessed, Darcy claimed, to possession of the four familiars – two female spirits that brought sickness to people and destroyed cattle and two male spirits that killed people.

Also naming another twelve women as witches, she was hanged along with five of them – victims of the truly deadly superstitions of their time.

A further twist to the grim tale came nearly 340 years later, in 1921, when the skeletons of two women, one believed to be Ursula Kemp, were unearthed from a garden in her home village of St Osyth.

Put on display for a time as 'the witches' skeletons' and with an admission charge to view them, recent forensic examination however suggests the bones are of much earlier, pre-Roman period, provenance.

Chapter three:

Grand designs

Not only a soldier, businessman and politician but also a talented sportsman, George Kemp, 1st Baron Rochdale, was born in the Lancashire town from which he took his title in 1866.

Graduating with a degree in classics from Cambridge University when aged 22, he served during the Second Boer War of 1899 to 1902 as a captain of the Imperial Yeomanry and, during the First World War, as a lieutenant-colonel in command of the 1st/6th Battalion, Lancashire Fusiliers and as a brigadier general during the battle of Gallipoli in 1915.

As a businessman, he entered the woollen industry and became chairman of the Lancashire flannel manufacturers Kelsall and Kemp.

First elected to Parliament as Liberal Unionist MP (Member of Parliament) for Heywood and, in 1895, as the Liberal member for Manchester North West, government posts he held included Parliamentary Secretary to the Admiralty while, in opposition to his own party, he was firmly aginst Irish Home Rule.

Elevated to the peerage as 1st Baron

Rochdale, as a young man he had excelled in sport as a lawn tennis 'Blue' for his university and in first-class cricket as a batsman for his home county Lancashire.

He died in 1945, while through his marriage to Lady Beatrice Egerton, daughter of Francis Egerton, 3rd Earl of Ellesmere, he was the father of the soldier, businessman and peer Brigadier John Durval Kemp, 1st Viscount Rochdale.

Serving throughout the Second World War with the British Army in India and also for a time with U.S. Forces in the Pacific, in business the brigadier was chairman of the family firm Kelsall and Kemp from 1950 to 1971, while also representing a number of outside bodies.

This included the presidency from 1953 to 1956 of the National Union of Manufacturers, chairmanship of the Cotton Board from 1957 to 1962 and, from 1954 to 1959, as chairman of the BBC.

Having succeeded to the barony of Rochdale on his father's death and later elevated to the peerage as 1st Viscount Rochdale, he died in 1993.

Although a politician, it was as a property developer that Thomas Read Kemp left a legacy that survives to this day on the landscape of the English south coast resort of Brighton.

Born in 1782, the son of a Sussex landowner, he studied law and then entered politics as MP for Lewes from 1811 to 1816 and then, from 1823 to 1826, for the Arundel constituency.

But it was as a property developer that he conceived and financed the Regency-style Kemptown residential estate in Brighton.

Designed by Amon Henry Wilds and Charles Busby and built by Thomas Cubitt, work on what was then the biggest housing crescent in Britain began in 1823.

But, landing heavily in debt, Kemp had to flee from Britain to escape his creditors in 1837, dying in penury in Paris seven years later.

Work on his grand concept had carried on, however, and with the help of funding from the fifth Earl of Bristol was completed in 1855.

The development – featuring Arundel Terrace, Chichester Terrace, Lewes Crescent and Sussex Square and one of the jewels in the crown of Brighton – now forms part of the Kemptown district of the town.

From building to gardens, Edward Kemp was the English landscape architect and author born in 1817 in Streatham, Surrey.

The son of a tailor, he was apprenticed as a gardener at Chatsworth House, Derbyshire, working under Edward Milner and, in 1843, was appointed by the authorities in Birkenhead, Merseyside, to plan and construct Birkenhead Park.

The first of its kind in Britain provided at public expense, work on the park was completed four years later and Kemp appointed its superintendent.

In addition to this duty he also undertook a number of other commissions including the design of the rose garden in the grounds of Lymm Hall, Cheshire, Grosvenor Park, also Chester and Queen's Park, in Crewe.

The author of books including the influential 1850 *How to Lay Out a Small Garden*, he died in 1891.

North of the border, George Meikle Kemp was the Scottish self-taught architect who, against all odds, became responsible for one of Edinburgh's most iconic landmarks.

Despite his humble background and resistance from the architectural establishment, he designed and built the famous Scott Monument in the capital's Princes Street.

Born in 1795 at Hillriggs Farm, above the town of Biggar, Lanarkshire, his father was a 'herd', or shepherd, and the family of six children had frequently to resort to poor relief in order to keep body and soul together.

After a very brief formal education, he was aged only 11 when he joined his father in the hills as a shepherd, constantly moving from farm to farm in search of work.

But in childhood he showed an uncanny understanding of all things mechanical and also a highly creative artistic streak and, when aged, 14, was apprenticed as a joiner near Peebles, in the Borders.

Studying hard at night and also walking long distances to view examples of the Gothic architecture that fascinated him – such as the Border abbeys of Melrose, Kelso, Dryburgh and Jedburgh and the mysterious Rosslyn Chapel, in Midlothian, he later worked for a time in Manchester repairing mill machinery.

Returning to his native land, he attended evening classes in geometry, draughtsmanship and science at Anderson's Institution in Glasgow, forerunner of the University of Strathclyde.

Ever restless and in search of employment, he worked for a time in London utilising his mechanical skills and also visiting and studying Gothic masterpieces such as Westminster Abbey.

Returning to Scotland in 1827 he set up in business in Edinburgh as a cabinet-maker – but the course of his life changed dramatically in 1836 when a 'committee of noblemen and gentlemen' launched a competition to design a monument in honour of the great antiquarian and novelist Sir Walter Scott, who had died four years previously.

A number of leading architects had already been invited to submit designs but, with none of them proving satisfactory, the competition was set in motion with a prize of 50 guineas each for the best three designs.

Rising to the challenge and utilising his vast knowledge of Gothic architecture, Kemp produced a finished design in only five days – submitting it under the pseudonym 'John Morvo' – the name of the French master mason who had worked on the building of both Melrose Abbey and Rosslyn Chapel.

Of the 54 entries, his was one of the three chosen – but controversy erupted when it was discovered 'John Morvo' was in fact the 'untrained' architect George Meikle Kemp.

That 'someone so unqualified, inexperienced

and obscure, and not even an architect' should have been one of the winners was a travesty, thundered not only the aggrieved losers but also the other two winners.

The competition organisers nevertheless stuck to their guns and decided to choose from the three winning designs but, unable to reach a decision, launched the scheme again.

Established architects again submitted their ideas but it was Kemp, this time under his own name and with a modified design, who was chosen.

The committee praised what it described as "an imposing structure, 135ft (41 metres) in height, of beautiful proportions, and in strict conformity with the purity and taste of Melrose Abbey, from which the author states is in all its details derived."

With Kemp appointed Clerk of Works for the building project, the foundation stone for the Scott Monument was laid on August 15, 1840, the 69th anniversary of the writer's birth and the day declared a public holiday.

Kemp, popular with the workmen who laboured on the project and members of the public who saw him day after day tirelessly overseeing operations, tragically never lived to see its completion.

While walking home on the foggy night of March 6, 1844 after meeting his builder, he drowned in the Union Canal, his body found a few days later in the Lochrin Basin, at Fountainbridge – whether by foul play or accident has never been determined.

Amidst a great outpouring of public grief, his coffin was carried by workmen from his home in Morningside to St Cuthbert's churchyard, below the castle, where he lies buried in the southern section – rather aptly facing the monument he designed.

With its original planned height increased to 200ft 6inches (61.11 metres), work was completed only a few months after his death, with his 10-year-old son Thomas placing the topmost stone.

With a vast crowd attending the official inauguration ceremony on August 15, 1846, the Scott Monument stands in splendour to this day as not only a fitting memorial to the writer himself, but also to its creator George Meikle Kemp, the humble shepherd lad.

Chapter four:

On the world stage

Musicians, singers, songwriters, actors and directors, Gary and Martin Kemp are the brothers best known as members of the British band of the 1980s Spandau Ballet.

Born to a working class family in Islington, London in 1959, Gary Kemp was the band's lead guitarist and principal songwriter while his brother, born in 1961, was bass guitarist.

With the addition of Tony Hadley as vocalist and synthesiser player, Steve Norman on guitar and John Keeble on drums, the band enjoyed a string of international hits including *Gold*, *True*, *To Cut a Long Story Short* and *Chant No.1 (I Don't Need This Pressure On)*.

Having split up on a number of occasions they reformed briefly in 2009, while Gary Kemp was the recipient in 2012 of an Ivor Novello Award for Outstanding Song Collection.

As actors, the brothers starred together in the 1990 film *The Krays*, based on the London gangsters of the name, with Gary in the role of Ronald (Ronnie)

Kray and Martin as his twin brother Reginald (Reggie).

Gary Kemp has also appeared on the big screen in films including the 1992 *The Bodyguard*, while Martin played the villain Steve Owen in the BBC television soap *EastEnders*, winning a number of awards for the role including the 2000 National Television Award for Most Popular Actor.

Other television credits include *The Bill* and the drama *The Brides in the Bath*, in which he played the English serial killer and bigamist George Smith, while in 2020 he and his brother starred in the television comedy spoof of their lives *The Kemps: All True*.

Known for his association with the British folk rock band Steeleye Span and his own successful solo career, **Rick Kemp** is the English guitarist, vocalist, songwriter and producer born in 1941 in Little Hanford, Dorset.

Having first joined the band in 1972 and performed with them over a number of years, enjoying hits including *Gaudette* and *All Around My Hat*, through his former marriage to Steeleye Span lead vocalist Maddy Prior he is the father of the singer and guitarist **Rose Kemp**, born in Carlisle in 1984.

Influenced by a number of music genres, her solo albums include the acoustic pop *Glance*.

Across the Atlantic, **James Hal Kemp** was a leading early twentieth century American jazz alto saxophonist, clarinettist, bandleader, composer and arranger.

Born in 1904 in Marion, Alabama, he formed his own band that featured other jazz greats including John Scott Trotter, Bunny Berigan and Skinnay Ennis.

Enjoying a number of hits including *Lullaby of Broadway*, *In the Middle of a Kiss* and *When I'm With You*, he was killed in 1940 while driving from Los Angeles to a performance in San Francisco when his car was struck by an oncoming truck.

On the stage, **Ross Kemp**, born in 1964 in Barking, Essex is the actor, presenter, investigative journalist and author known for his intermittent role between 1990 and 2016 of Grant Mitchell in *EastEnders*.

In addition to other television credits including *London's Burning* and the 2002 *Ultimate Force*, as a journalist he has fronted hard-hitting documentaries that include the BAFTA Award-winning *Ross Kemp on Gangs*, *Ross Kemp in Afghanistan* and *Ross Kemp: Extreme World*.

In 2005 he and his then wife Rebekah Wade, then editor of the *Sun* newspaper were the subject of headlines when Wade was arrested after allegedly assaulting him in their home.

But charges were not pressed, while the couple divorced in 2009.

With both television and big screen credits, Edmund Jeremy James Walker was the English actor better known by his stage name **Jeremy Kemp**, born in 1935 in Chesterfield, Derbyshire.

His television credits include *Colditz*, *The Winds of War*, *Remembrance* and *Star Trek: The Next Generation*, while major films include the 1966 *The Blue Max*, the 1977 *A Bridge Too Far* and, fifteen years before his death in 2019, *Four Weddings and a Funeral*.

Born in Oxford in 1965, **Edward Kemp** is a noted playwright and theatre director.

Appointed director of the Royal Academy of Dramatic Art (RADA) in 2008 and principal of its umbrella institution the Conservatoire for Dance and Drama in 2014, his play *5/11*, premiered at the Chichester Festival Theatre in 2005, marked the 400th anniversary of the Gunpowder Plot of 1605.

Bearers of the Kemp name have also excelled in the highly competitive world of sport.

In the swimming pool, Jennifer Jo Kemp, better known as **Jenny Kemp**, is the American former competitor, born in 1955 in Cincinnati, who won a gold medal in the 4x100-meter freestyle relay at the 1972 Olympics.

Both a New Zealand association football player and a cricketer, **John Kemp** was born in Auckland in 1940.

The holder of four international caps playing football for his nation, before his death in 1993 he had also played 25 matches between 1960 and 1970 for Auckland Cricket Association.

Also in New Zealand, **Tony Kemp** is the former rugby league player and coach born in 1968 in Whangarei.

An internationalist and a former coach of the New Zealand Warriors, clubs he played for include South Queensland Crushers and English teams Castleford Tigers and Newcastle Knights.

From the rugby pitch to the skating rink, Stacey King is the married name of the English former competitive pair skater **Stacey Kemp**, born in 1988 in Preston, Lancashire.

Along with her then skating partner and now husband David King she became an eight-time British national champion, while the couple also competed at Olympic and World Championship level.

In another artistic discipline, **Lindsay Kemp** was the British dancer, actor, mime artist, choreographer and teacher born in 1938 in Birkenhead, Merseyside.

Producer of a number of operatic works and a dancer in films including the 1976 *Sebastiane* and the 1977 *Jubilee*, he was also an inspirational teacher of artistes including David Bowie and Kate Bush.

Bowie's 1972 London performances of his *Ziggy Stardust* persona were staged by Kemp, while the Kate Bush song *Moving* was written as a tribute to him; he died in 2018.

In the equally creative world of the written word, **Anthony Kemp** was the distinguished British historian and journalist born in London in 1939.

Specialising in military history, particularly the Second World War, he was the author of works including *Allied Commanders of World War II*, *German Commanders of World War II* and *The SAS at War, 1941-1945*.

Also an authority on paganism and witchcraft and the author of works including the 1995 *Witchcraft and Paganism Today*, he died in 2018.

In art, Jacobina Kemp, better known as **Jeka Kemp**, was the Scottish artist famed for her woodcut and watercolour paintings of landscapes and street scenes.

Born in 1876 in the Bellahouston district of Glasgow and mainly self-taught, she travelled widely throughout Europe and North Africa for inspiration.

Having exhibited in institutions including the Royal Scottish Academy, Royal Glasgow Institute of Fine Arts and with the Societe National des Beaux-Arts, Paris, she died in 1966 and has since been the subject of a number of retrospective exhibitions.

A leading authority on the work of Leonardo da Vinci, **Martin Kemp**, born in 1942, is the distinguished British professor of the history of art with a rather unusual claim to fame.

Having studied the many hundreds of sketches made by the highly inventive artistic genius, he advised the daring skydiver Adrian Nicholas on how to construct a parachute based on drawings made by da Vinci and using only materials that would have been available in his day.

An intriguing sketch from 1485 shows a four-sided pyramid covered in linen and with the accompanying note:

If a man is provided with a length of gummed linen cloth with a length of 12 yards on each side and 12 yards high, he can jump from any great height whatsoever without injury.

Following da Vinci's plan a parachute was constructed and, in June of 2000, Nicholas jumped from a hot air balloon 10,000ft (3,000m) over South Africa.

Parachuting for five minutes with the da Vinci-designed 'chute, he then cut himself free from the device and, deploying a conventional parachute, landed safely.

The descent of the first parachute had been so slow and smooth that two skydivers who had accompanied Nicholas had to 'brake' twice to stay level with him.

Kemp, meanwhile, a former professor at both St Andrews and Glasgow universities and emeritus professor at Oxford University, has staged a number of exhibitions that include, in 2006 at the Victoria and Albert Museum, London, *Leonardo da Vinci: Experience, Experiment, Design*.